The Way of the Dolphin

The Way of the Dolphin

Dr. Michael Fox

Illustrated by Betty J. Lewis

ACROPOLIS BOOKS LTD.
Washington, D.C. 20009

Copyright © 1981 by Acropolis Books

All rights reserved. Except for the inclusion of brief quotations in a review, no part of this book may be reproduced or utilized in any form or by any means, electronic or mechanical, including photocopying, recording or by an information storage and retrieval system, without permission in writing from the publisher.

ACROPOLIS BOOKS LTD.
Colortone Building, 2400 17th St., N.W.
Washington, D.C. 20009

Printed in the United States of America by
COLORTONE PRESS, Creative Graphics Inc.
Washington, D.C. 20009

Library of Congress Cataloging in Publication Data

```
Fox, Michael W., 1937-
   The way of the dolphin.

   Summary: Discusses the habitat and behavior of
dolphins, presenting some experiences such as birth
of, escape from a school of killer whales, and
cavorting with a fisherman and his son.
   1. Dolphins--Juvenile literature.  [1. Dolphins]
I. Title.
QL737.C432F69      599.5'3        81-12743
ISBN 0-87491-466-3                 AACR2
```

Dedication

For my daughter Camilla and to our cousins of the seas

The Way Of The Dolphin

CONTENTS

	Introduction............................11
	Animals of the Sea 12
Chapter 1	The Dolphin Band 15
Chapter 2	Ocean Birth....................21
Chapter 3	Sea-School......................29
Chapter 4	The Search For Food 37
Chapter 5	Trapped By A Net 45
Chapter 6	Boy On A Dolphin 53
Chapter 7	Killer Cousins 61
Chapter 8	Tragedy And Discovery 69
Chapter 9	The Giant Net 77
	Postscript 85
	Dolphin Anatomy 88
	Dolphin Sonar 90
	Cycle Of Ocean Life...........92
	Glossary 94

The Way Of The Dolphin

Plutarch, the Greek philosopher, sang these words of praise to the dolphin some 2,500 years ago:

"On the dolphin,
alone among all others,
Nature has bestowed this gift
which the greatest philosophers long for:
disinterested friendship.
It has no need of any man,
yet it is the friend of all men
and has often given them
great aid."

The Way Of The Dolphin

Some Animals of the Sea

Shark 15'

Giant Squid 50'

Gray Whale 50'

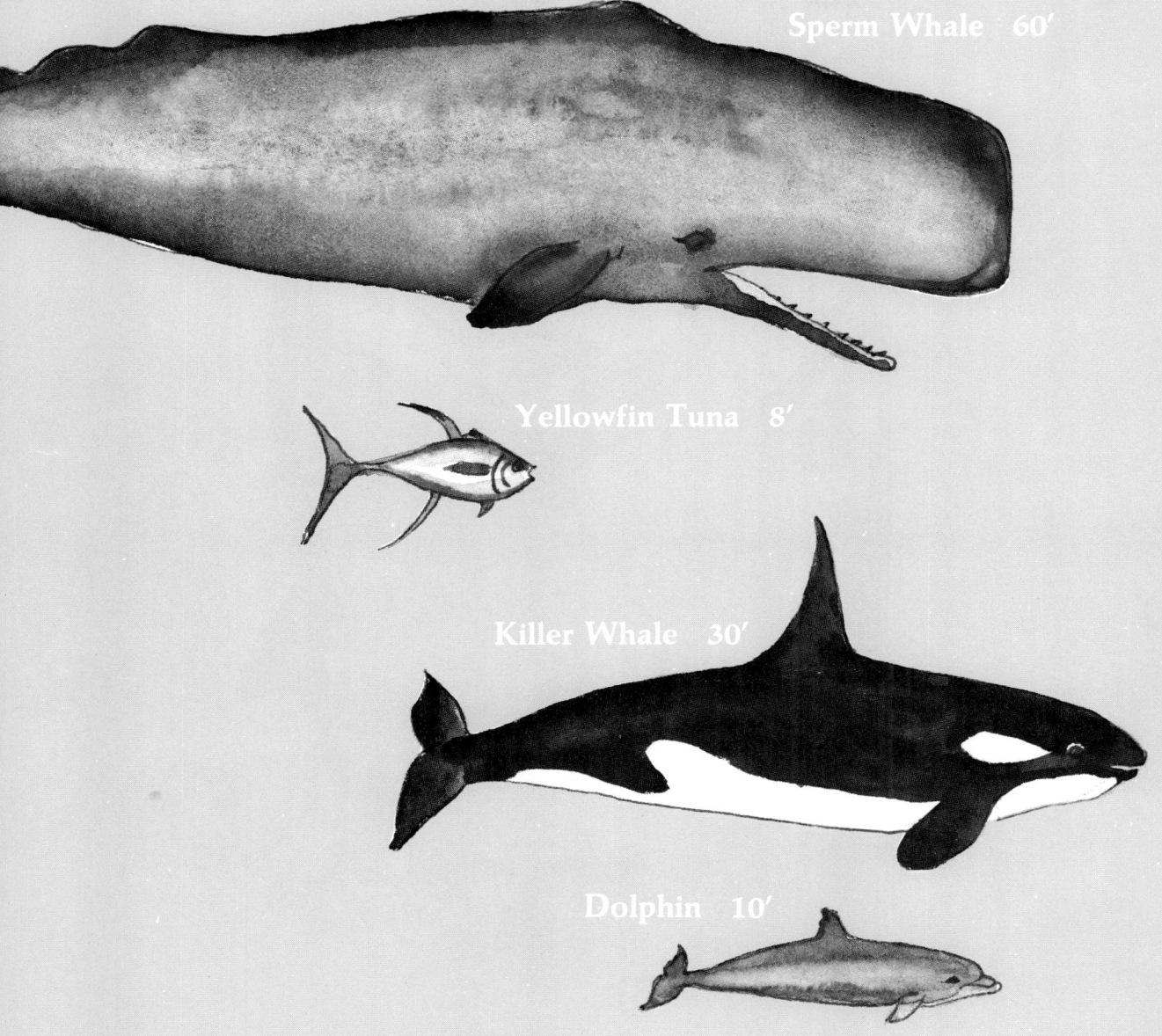

The Way Of The Dolphin

INTRODUCTION

Since the beginning of recorded history, dolphins have been admired as symbols of freedom and perfection, for good reason. They embody grace, intelligence, fearlessness, kinship, altruism; in fact, all of those qualities we regard as the most desirable of human virtues are found in them. For this reason, some might say dolphins are the people of the sea. They share much with us, but they have much to teach us. What dolphins can share with us can make us more compassionate and concerned for all creatures, great and small, of the sea, land and sky. Their story is important to all of us. Unless we care about the dolphins who remain in another generation, there may be no more dolphins left for us to learn from.

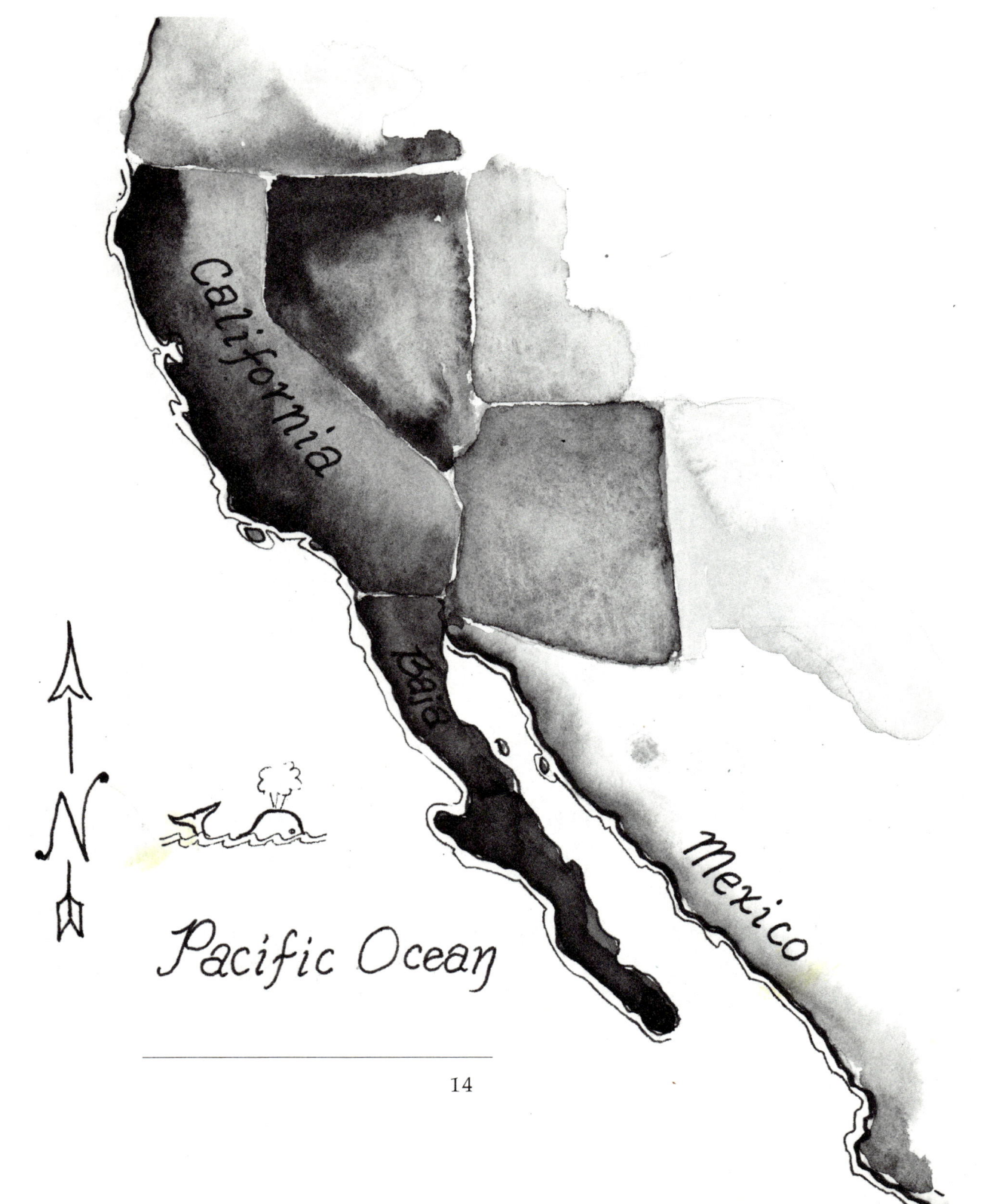

CHAPTER ONE

The Dolphin Band

The light grew darker as they slipped down, down through the layers of ocean, down from the pale green, through the deep emerald and then into the cold blue-purple. Deeper still lay the ever colder blackness of a thousand fathoms. Their bodies moved easily under a weight of water that would have crushed creatures that have not lived in the ocean, as their dolphin ancestors had, for a million years.

They found the deep current that flowed like a strong river between cliffs of water and allowed it to carry them along. Soon, they would be swept into the main current that would take them in a vast arc under the warm, salty, Pacific waters, along the coast of California to the Baja Peninsula, then to the coast of Mexico beyond. Every ten or fifteen minutes, they rose together slowly to take in deep breaths of fresh air and, after a few leaps and dives on the surface, plunge again into the deeper current that carried them so far and so easily.

They were bottle-nosed dolphins and they moved as if they were one with the sea, as though they had become part of its

color and movement after thousands of generations of evolution. The sea had nurtured them, shaped their flippers and flukes to ease their travel in the water, streamlined their bodies until they had become perfectly sculptured for high speed movement and agility in the water.

Teeka, the lead dolphin, whistled "Teeka-Teeka" and the six behind him responded, calling out their names in return. In the deep current, the sounds would dart ahead of them for miles, announcing their arrival to other dolphins swimming on ocean paths of their own.

Teeka began to rise. Soon, all seven felt the warmth of sunlight and the lightness of the surface as they burst upwards into the air to breathe. A flying fish skimmed by, alarmed by their sudden appearance. One, two, three—each dived, surfaced alternately, then together. Teeka set the pace and rhythm. As

they rose and fell in harmony, each a mirror image of the next, they suddenly found themselves joined by others. Teeka's band mingled with these four who had been ahead of them, rolling and rubbing backs and bellies, squeaking and rubbing their beaklike noses in greeting. Then they moved as a single body once again, dolphins diving and rising together in rhythm with the rise and fall of the waves, at one with the sea.

The Way Of The Dolphin

CHAPTER TWO

Ocean Birth

Teeka began to swim in a circle, signaling to the whole school to slow down. They formed a tight circle around his mate Tiktik, preparing instinctively for the birth of one of their own kind.

Tiktik had already passed a small amount of fluid into the sea from the sac that was breaking inside her body. Inside the sac her first young had been nurtured and, as it slowly grew, Tiktik's sides had swelled until the movements of the infant inside her could be seen and felt by the other dolphins. Their wonderful sense of sonar "x-ray vision," which allowed them to see underwater, had let them know that Tiktik was ready to give birth.

From the fluid in the water, four large sharks had also sensed that Tiktik was to give birth; they were circling close to the protective wall of dolphins that separated them from Tiktik.

The dolphins anxiously monitored the presence of the waiting sharks with their sonar apparatus. Sousou, the experienced matron dolphin of the group, kept close to Tiktik, rubbing her body against the other dolphin with tender reassurance. The baby would be born soon.

Suddenly, the largest shark darted forward, testing the defensive wall the dolphins had made. Teeka turned sideways and extended his flippers, to challenge the shark. The shark veered away, his eyes focused on Teeka. Sousou caught the shark unaware—she darted forward and struck him with her powerful nose in the softest part of his body.

As the shark twisted to bite at her, Sousou fearlessly rammed his unguarded flank. Eight hundred pounds of dolphin charging into a shark's soft belly were too much for the tiger of the sea. Confused by the two attackers, the great shark slipped away into the dark ocean beneath, the rest of the sharks close behind him. The dolphins had neither the powerful teeth nor

Ocean Birth

The Way Of The Dolphin

jaws of the shark, but they had the great advantages of intelligence, sonar "vision" and mutual cooperation to use as weapons against their enemies.

With the shark danger past, the dolphins began to chatter and surge around Tiktik until the water was white with foam. Her baby had been born in the midst of the shark attack.

Tiktik and Sousou supported the infant with their noses to hold it above the water as it squeaked and took its first breaths. Each dolphin rubbed the new member of the school with its body, squeaking its name and amid the excited and friendly chatter of the others.

Tiktik's infant was soon responding to the other dolphins in high-pitched little squeaks, repeating his own distinct call. It sounded like "Nick-Nick," and, the more he repeated it, the clearer it became. Later, how and when he said it would have all kinds of meanings to the other dolphins, from "I'm over here" or "It's me" to "Help me" or "I'm coming."

Gently, Sousou and Tiktik pulled away from Nick-Nick and he splashed and twisted in front of them. He was already an accomplished swimmer. He took a deep breath and dived down towards his mother, twisting his belly to rub against hers. It felt good, and his body understood immediately the touching language of dolphins. Tiktik wiggled against Nick-Nick and he responded by rubbing against her. Then, she moved over him and turned onto her side so that his beak rested against her. The sea water close to his mouth tasted good; instinctively, Nick-Nick lunged forward to find the source of that rich, sweet taste. He bumped one of his mother's teats, and instinctively, he began to suck. He was rewarded immediately as milk was injected into his mouth by special muscles that surrounded his mother's teats. For his first two or three weeks, he would nurse every half hour, then, at longer intervals until he was a year or more of age.

Nick-Nick had taken the first great step in life; the sudden rush of birth from a warm, secure world inside his mother into the colder world within the vast ocean. He had taken his first breath, a ritual held over from the dolphin's prehistoric existence as a land animal but, now, only an echo of the past. His ties now were with the sea and his kin.

After his meal, Nick-Nick lay half sleeping against his mother's side. The ocean rocked with the same rhythm he had felt inside his mother, but the cool waves and cold air in the nostril blow hole on top of his head made him aware of himself for the first time. As he was a part of all things, so, too, he seemed to be at the center of life. "Nick-Nick, Nick-Nick," he squeaked. Then, he fell asleep.

CHAPTER THREE

Sea-School

During the first month of his life, Nick-Nick never left his mother's side. Sometimes, when he began to dash off, Tiktik would discipline him with a prod from her beak. Nick-Nick was even more curious and playful than most young dolphins, and Sousou, knowing this, usually kept close to Tiktik to help her with her unruly infant. Sometimes, a brightly colored jellyfish or a swarm of shrimplike krill would attract Nick-Nick's attention and he would leap out of the protective circle of his mother's body, away from her shoulder. Within seconds, he would find himself lifted by Sousou's beak and propelled at great speed in a circle, back to his mother. Although he was unable to escape, Nick-Nick enjoyed

these speed rides. They were worth the occasional prod from Tiktik's beak he received on his return.

Life near his protective and loving mother wasn't that bad for Nick-Nick. The two of them would spend long hours in the afternoon rolling and twisting as they swam together. Tiktik taught Nick-Nick many dolphin games that would later help him make friends with other dolphins.

One game Nick-Nick called "spinning" was one of his favorites. He would try to stay as close as possible to Tiktik's dorsal, or top, fin as she twisted and rolled at high speed under the water. Sometimes, Nick-Nick would try to escape past his mother in a high-spirited game of "tag." Tiktik would race around him at high speed, twisting and turning to block him

Sea School

The Way Of The Dolphin

from escaping past her. Sometimes, she would allow him to escape, and he would dive as fast as he could, trying to keep far enough from her so she couldn't touch his hind flippers or flukes. Then Nick-Nick would chase her.

Nick-Nick's very favorite game was "pat-a-cake." Either he or Tiktik would swim under the other, twisting with belly up, touching the flippers of the dolphin on top. They raced faster and faster, spinning in a great spiral, one over the other. Nick-Nick rejoiced in moving his agile body through water, mimicking the actions of his mother and the other dolphins in a way much like that of human dancers, only faster and more perfectly coordinated. Although he was only playing, he always had his sonar apparatus in operation so he could sense the sonar patterns that his mother received and transmitted and those of the other dolphins as well. In this way, he was always aware of what the others felt, saw and knew.

Nick-Nick had to spend many months close to his mother because he had a great deal to learn—all the names and signals of the other dolphins in their family and the family's common language. He had to learn to use his second sonar apparatus to make "x-ray" pictures and learn exactly what the sonar echo pictures meant, *and* he had to master dolphin language—all at the same time!

First, he learned to see the sound pictures that his mother was seeing by tuning in to the echos from her sonar. Then, as their minds and senses became more tuned to each other, he found he was given more freedom. Unlike a human infant who becomes more independent as he or she matures, Nick-Nick became, as he grew, more and more like the other dolphins in his family. Once he was full-grown, he would be able to swim, dive and play with other dolphins, matching his movements to theirs, just as though they were one. They all felt and sensed what the others close to them were experiencing; all were tuned in to each other and to the ocean in a remarkable way.

One day, Teeka came over to Tiktik and nuzzled her gently. Nick-Nick was ready to go with his father to the front of the school, to learn to hunt and acquire the great knowledge that dolphins pass on to each other, from one generation to the next.

The Way Of The Dolphin

CHAPTER FOUR

The Search For Food

The dolphins cruised easily over the surface of the water, going further and further away from the shore and further into the deep ocean. When they had come to an area where the deep, surging current was very strong, Nick-Nick felt and tasted a change in the water. The water swelling up from the depths brought with it decayed material, called ooze, from the bottom of the ocean. The ooze was food for the trillions of microscopic plants and animals, called plankton, that multiplied in these waters, creating a rich "soup" of nutrients. The plankton was consumed by microscopic creatures—krill, baby crabs and jellyfish—who, were eaten by small fish, part of the never-ending cycle of ocean life.

Teeka soon located a school of mackerel and many schools of mullet, their favorite food. Nick-Nick quickly learned to sense the differences among the various kinds of fish by using his sonar apparatus. The fish could not hear the dolphin's sonar beams—it was a sound too high-pitched for their ears—and they were easy for the dolphins to approach.

Teeka signaled the others. They began to swim in a tight and shrinking circle around the fish, pulling them into a small ball of flashing silver pieces. Nick-Nick saw Sousou and two other dolphins, flipper to flipper, dive into the fish ball with their mouths wide open. After they had fed, they joined the circle that formed the dolphins' "net," and it was Nick-Nick's turn to dive into the fish with Teeka.

Once they had eaten their fill, the dolphins played. Teeka showed his son how to skate on the surface of the water by leaping out and propelling himself backward with his flukes.

The Search For Food

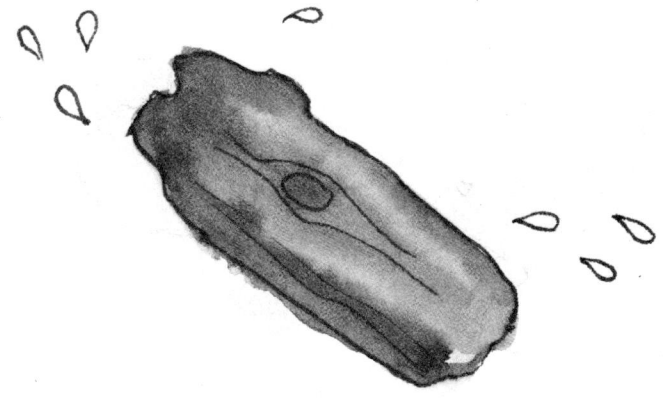

Nick-Nick quickly caught on and enjoyed standing up and racing backward over the water. Later, he and the other dolphins played water polo with a soggy piece of floating driftwood. Teeka could run at high speed balancing the driftwood on his nose; the others tried to stop him from racing off with the prize. Once, when Teeka flipped the wood toward Nick-Nick, the young dolphin's sonar picked up something enormous looming just beyond the frolicking dolphins. He sensed what seemed to be a high, floating island in front of him!

The school circled the great mass. To Nick-Nick's surprise, they talked to it and it talked back! It was Kraakaan, a solitary bull sperm whale. He rolled gently, stroking his great flukes and flippers over the dolphins who were all crowded around him. Nick-Nick saw the whale's great eye and drew closer, sensing the friendliness radiating from the whale's body and sonar communication.

In good humor, the whale blew a great spume of sea and air through his blow hole and dived past Nick-Nick. A great diver, Kraakaan, was hunting for giant squid that abounded in the depths of this rich part of the Pacific Ocean.

Kraakaan was one of the last of his kind. Men had hunted his kin for centuries for meat, oil and valuable ambergris, used in perfumes, until there were few whales remaining.

Nick-Nick knew none of this. He knew only that the great bull was lonely. Although he stayed with the dolphin band for several days, fishing, talking and touching, Kraakaan finally left them. With a great slapping of his flukes and a sounding from his blow hole, he bid them good-bye. Teeka and the others squeaked and played in the huge wake, the wave of water left as he dove, then they, too, departed. They returned to the familiar coastline south of Baja, home.

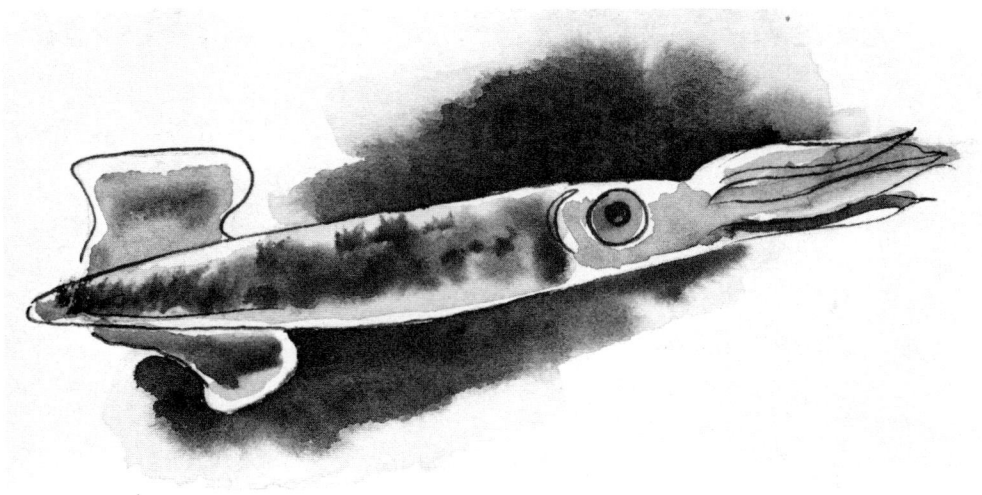

The Way Of The Dolphin

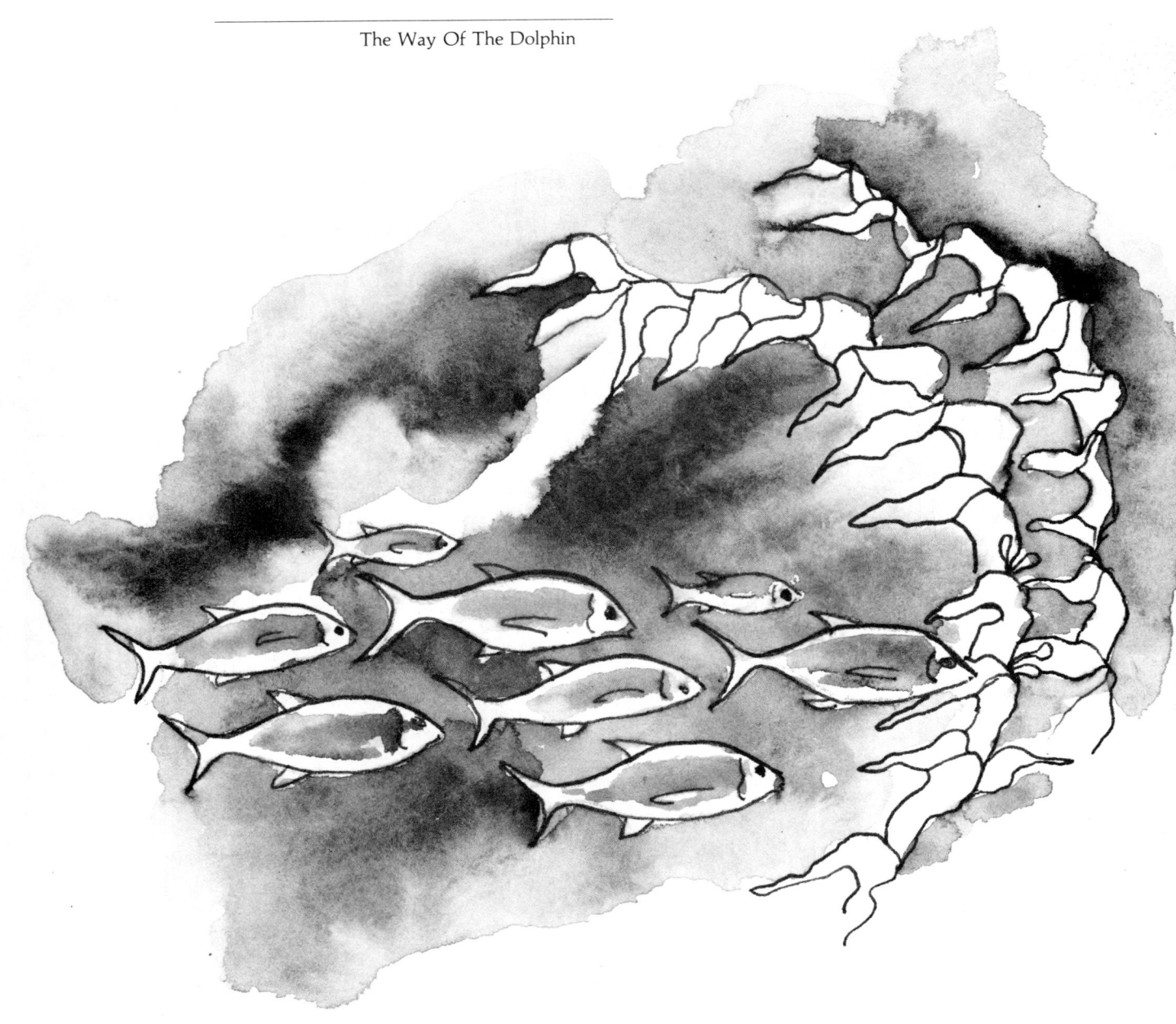

CHAPTER FIVE

Trapped By A Net

Nick-Nick grew fast and strong under the watchful eyes of the other dolphins. Sometimes, the band roamed the open seas; other times, they hugged the warm, blue coastal waters around Baja and Mexico. Nick-Nick learned to stay with the school and not stray or lag behind, even when his curiosity tried to get the better of him. The strength and survival of the dolphins depended upon their acting with one mind in all things.

One night, after feeding on a school of mackerel in a lagoon not far from shore, the dolphins were playing together in the quiet waters. The surface of the water was bright with tiny, light-emitting or phosphorescent plankton that covered the dolphins' backs and sides as they dove and swam. The dolphins were delighted with the beautiful brightness the plankton gave them, and they paid Nick-Nick little attention as he strayed away from them.

Nick-Nick had found a coconut floating far from land. He began to play dolphin soccer, striking and flipping the coconut up in the air with his beak, good practice for driving off sharks. His solitary game led him further and further away from the others. Suddenly, he could not reach the coconut nor could he turn one way or the other. He expanded his field of sonar vision until he could sense fine strands all around him. He did not panic, for, like a human swimmer in distress, he could have drowned. Instead, he sent out the dolphin distress whistle and called, "Nick-Nick! Nick-Nick!" Within seconds, he heard the others, coming to his rescue. He felt long, thin patterns of pressure over his chest and head which grew tighter whenever he moved. Soon, he would have to rise to the surface to take a breath.

Trapped By A Net

Suddenly, he felt dolphin noses under his belly, pushing him, guiding him, but they could not free him from the strands holding him prisoner. There was no way out.

Fishermen trying to catch small fish drawn by the tide and full moon to spawn on the shores had spread their nets in the lagoon. Seeing the dolphins' gleaming bodies surrounding their nets, the fishermen rowed closer. Sousou rose into the air, crying "Eeek—Eeek."

Trapped By A Net

The village fishermen seemed to understand her distress. Quickly, they pulled the net into their boat and rolled Nick-Nick free onto the deck. He gasped for breath and squeaked in terror as he felt their warm hands on his skin. The strong odors of wood, pitch tar, fish and the sour-sweetness of man flooded his tongue, his taste and smell organ. He looked up and sideways to see huge eyes and white teeth shining at him. "Eeek—Eeek," he cried in alarm. The other dolphins struck the hull of the boat with their beaks, trying to help him. One fisherman smiled in sympathy, but Nick-Nick didn't know the meaning of a smile. Not having any facial expressions himself, how could he know the fisherman meant him no harm?

But, then, he felt the soft, warm touch along his side as one of the fishermen stroked him tenderly, and he heard a young boy laugh, a sound not unlike the play chatter of dolphin talk.

He tried to laugh back, but his fear made his voice crack, "Eeek-Eeek, Eeek-Eeek," and, at the sound, the other dolphins struck the boat with their beaks. The fishermen gently dropped Nick-Nick back into the water. All the dolphins squeaked, beating the water into foam around him. Then, one of the fishermen, the young boy who had laughed, slipped into the water with the dolphins.

The Way Of The Dolphin

CHAPTER SIX

Boy On A Dolphin

Two of the younger dolphins were alarmed and, diving, began to flee, but Tiktik's giggle greeting soon brought them back. The dolphins, sensing a friendly spirit, rubbed themselves over the boy and pushed him towards the surface of the water affectionately, as they would an infant dolphin. Sousou rolled over onto one side; the boy lay across her and, as she turned, he reached for her dorsal fin. As the boy held on, Sousou skimmed over the water around the boat, playfully pulling him along until he fell off. He swam back to the boat, the dolphins poking and pushing him gently on his journey. Then, all the dolphins circled the small boat, rising up

The Way Of The Dolphin

out of the water, clapping their jaws together and mewing happily. They could not feel the boy's tears of joy as he told his father about his wonderful experience, nor could they hear his father's response. "To be a fisherman, or anyone who has to kill animals for food, you must do what you have to do with respect; and sparingly, never taking more than you need. To be a good fisherman is to be a friend of the dolphin."

Nick-Nick knew that people could be kind. Hadn't the fishermen returned him to the sea? Perhaps, thought Nick-Nick, they are our kin. In the water, the boy's body had felt much as a dolphin's did. He had lungs like a dolphin's, Nick-Nick knew; he had sensed them with his sonar x-ray vision. "People of the sea," thought the boy. "Dolphins of the land," thought Nick-Nick.

To be a dolphin of the land, a man needed all kinds of machines, boats, nets, engines. Was life so hard on land? Wolves and eagles hadn't had to create such things to live well on earth. The dolphin needed nothing other than that which it had been given at birth to live a full and happy life in the ocean.

Perhaps when some of the early people of the land had moved to the sea, they found they no longer needed to create all those things in order to have a good life—perhaps they had become dolphins.

Perhaps, thought Nick-Nick, the boat took the place of the other dolphins pushing you up to the surface of the water so you could breathe and not drown. He had other dolphins to help him, so he had no need for a boat or net. The harmonious workings of their senses and bodies allowed them to catch fish with ease.

The dolphin needs no nets or boats to buy or build or keep in good repair, thought the boy, how free and beautiful is the way of the dolphin.

That night, the dolphins slept near the lagoon, going 'round and 'round in a slow circle on the surface of the water. Each had one eye open and the other closed for a few minutes at a time. Nick-Nick dreamed of his terrible experience in the net; his body twitched in sleep as he imagined the tight strands encircling him once again. Suddenly, he heard the "Eeek-Eeek" of Teeka and the other dolphins. The sleeping circle broke up and, in panic, they dived, crashing through the waves and swimming at top speed towards the shallows.

They had sensed that a pod, or family, of whales was crossing the mouth of the lagoon. These black and white killer whales, although intelligent and affectionate towards each other, would sometimes attack their cousins, the dolphins.

Nick-Nick would soon learn that his free life as a dolphin was possible only if he strictly obeyed the rules of his family and always used his sonar apparatus to detect the other, unseen creatures of the sea.

The Way Of The Dolphin

CHAPTER SEVEN

Killer Cousins

A huge bull whale broke from the pod and entered the lagoon, his sonar device quickly detecting the presence of the dolphins. His great, arched back-fin cut through the water. Teeka herded his family close to shore where they would be safe, for the killer whales would ground themselves in the shallow water. But one of the younger dolphins lost its nerve and headed for the deep waters outside the lagoon. Just what the killer whales were waiting for. Instantly, Sousou and Raana, his cousin, took off at great speed, hoping to lure the whale away from the terrified young dolphin. The bull struck at Teeka with his huge head, but before his teeth could slash him, the other dolphins rammed the whale's side.

He leaped out of the sea in pain and surprise, slapping his flukes to signal the other whales; within seconds, they were racing through the water towards their leader, then changing course to chase the dolphins into the deep ocean beyond the lagoon.

The smaller, faster dolphins wove and struck the more powerful, slower killer whales time and again. Finally, the whales gave up the hunt. Suddenly, they were gone, and the young, terrified dolphin was safe, and had learned a hard lesson.

Killer Cousins

The three dolphins rejoiced, but Sousou was silent. She began to sink slowly. Alarmed, Teeka and Raana pushed her up towards the surface, gently supporting her body where the whale had slashed a great wound in her side.

Slowly, moaning softly, Teeka and Raana pushed Sousou back to the lagoon. For six days and nights the dolphins stayed in the safety of the lagoon, taking turns supporting Sousou on the water's surface so she could breathe. After the third day, she had become weaker; on the fourth, she no longer responded to the gentle touches and loving sounds of her family. Then, she was no more: she had given her life willingly to save her family. For two days, they held her still body above the water.

Finally, Teeka sank slowly, mewing softly, and the others knew that it was time to give Sousou's body up to the ocean. They joined Teeka in quiet sadness, mourning their loss.

Sousou had been Teeka's older sister; he missed her deeply, not eating for several days. For the time being, Raana led the school; he took them to his favorite place along the bright, exciting coastline of southern California. Tiktik stayed close to Teeka on the journey, trying to coax him out of his sadness. Nick-Nick joined Raana in the lead and their spirits lifted as they drew closer to the lighter waters of the coast.

Nick-Nick could taste new elements in the current as they cruised north. He saw and felt the strange, waving beds of tall kelp, seaweed that grew like an endless forest close to shore. The barks and clacking noises of small, furry creatures drew him towards the kelp forest. When one of them dived off its floating bed into the water, Nick-Nick swam ahead to meet his first sea otter.

All the dolphins lingered at the edge of the seaweed, waiting to meet the otters. Although they had no sonar senses, the otters *were* warm-blooded, air-breathing kin, intelligent and playful.

Nick-Nick followed one otter diving for mussels and abalone, thick-shelled animals otters loved to eat. All the otters had to do was to roll onto their backs and crack the abalone shells open between two stones, just as though they were using a hammer and anvil.

Although the hungry sea otter broke off his food gathering briefly to play with Nick-Nick, he soon returned to his fishing. They could talk to each other only through body language and touch. Unlike dolphins, the sea otters had to find their food themselves, they did not have the senses or the group cooperation to hunt down schools of fish.

Suddenly, a loud explosion made the dolphins and sea otters dive together in alarm. Under water, Nick-Nick heard and felt the chung-chung-chung of an outboard motor. Men in boats again!

The Way Of The Dolphin

CHAPTER EIGHT

Tragedy And Discovery

The dolphins circled under the boat and they felt the loud noise again. Teeka, alarmed, kept his family out of sight under the water. How were they to know that these men were not like the friendly fishermen who had rescued Nick-Nick from the net? These were abalone fishermen, who did not wish to share their food with the sea otters. They were shooting at them when they came to the surface to breathe. The more experienced otters were hiding in the kelp, but some of the younger ones had instinctively gone into the deep water to escape and were now without a place to hide when they came up to breathe. The fishermen shot several of them.

Nick-Nick tried to save one of the wounded otters as he sank slowly in the water, but an "Eeek-Eeek," from Teeka and Raana drew him away. Teeka led the family back out to sea, away from death and the men in the boat.

After they had feasted on a school of mullet, Teeka seemed to regain his spirits and, calling to the others, he led them once again, diving deep to explore a long undersea ledge of sand. On one side was the deep ocean, on the other, a rising ridge of sand that seemed to stretch forever.

Tragedy And Discovery

Raana let out a bubble of air from his blow hole, an excited gurgle-pop of curiosity. The others turned towards him, fine-tuning their sonar apparatus to his. The buried wreck of an ancient boat rested on the edge of the sea ledge, half covered in sand.

In and out of the broken hull, around the broken masts, played the dolphins, constantly exploring the wreckage with their sonar devices and sharing their discoveries and feelings with each other. Nick-Nick carefully entered one broken hatch only to back out suddenly in surprise. Tiktik followed her son into the wreckage, emerging in a moment with the monster that had surprised Nick-Nick clasped in her beak.

    Calling to the others, Tiktik began to play with the eel (for that is what it was). The dolphins formed a circle and took turns tryng to catch the eel as it tried to return to its refuge in the dark belly of the wreck. Eventually, the dolphins allowed the eel to escape and, laughing together, they cruised off towards the open seas.

An albatross, a giant bird with great white wings, saw them and glided down, calling "Kee Naa, Kee Naa" as he effortlessly kept pace with them. Nick-Nick turned and twisted to see the bird more clearly. Although he had been followed and teased by gulls and other seabirds before, he had never seen a bird like this one. What was the spirit of the air with its giant wings? It seemed to encircle the world! He called to it, but it did not dive down into the water. A giant glider, the albatross finally soared away with a departing cry, "Kee Naa, Kee Naa!" What a wonderful bird, thought Nick-Nick. What a wonderful world!

He rose out of the water in great surging leaps, trying to fly like Kee Naa. On his third leap, he sensed what seemed to be a white wave of dancing lights racing towards him. Behind them was a large boat. He felt the throbbing engines as he dived and hurriedly tuned in to what the other dolphins were seeing and saying to each other. Ahead of them was a complex picture, indeed, one Nick-Nick could not, at first, understand.

A thousand dolphins were cruising together in a vast school, racing towards them like a hurricane tidal wave. Beneath them was a school of thousands of tuna, the fastest world travelers of all the fish.

The Way Of The Dolphin

CHAPTER NINE

The Giant Net

Raana and the other bottle-nosed dolphins signaled to the on-coming wave of their cousins. They couldn't wait to join them in a joyful reunion! The pull towards so many of their own kind was very strong, but Teeka turned away, snapping his jaws in alarm and lowering his head menacingly. He desperately tried to block Raana and his followers, to keep them from joining the others. Raana, enjoying the taste of leadership once more, ignored Teeka's warning. Tiktik obeyed her mate; she stopped Nick-Nick short with her powerful beak, pushing him upwards towards the ocean's surface as though he were an infant again. The three of them held back while the rest of the school raced ahead, following Raana.

Tiktik, Teeka, and Nick-Nick swam slowly nearer and sensed a great net surrounding the fish and dolphins. Speedboats churned and spun in tight circles over the water, keeping the dolphins and tuna in the back of the net that hung like a great curtain in the sea. Meanwhile, another boat pulled the net into a tightening circle. Once the net was closed, fishermen began to winch in the big cable that gathered the bottom of the net to close the trap. This took a long time, but, for some unknown reason, the fish and dolphins didn't think to swim out of the open bottom. Only a few escaped over the net.

Teeka and his family saw the net close like a purse. They sensed the terror and confusion of the dolphins trapped in the net. Tuna and dolphin bodies were crushed together as the net grew tighter. The beautiful dolphin reunion was ending in a nightmare of broken, drowning bodies and a thousand distress calls.

Suddenly, the ocean was silent as the net was pulled up out of the water and into the boat.

The Giant Net

Teeka, Tiktik and Nick-Nick drew closer to the boat as dolphin bodies were thrown back into the sea by the fishermen. Many were dead. Others, injured or half-drowned, were too many for them to rescue.

With their sonar, the family located Raana. He was still alive. They pushed him away from the boat and supported him while he tried to breathe. They could sense that his chest had been crushed and that his lungs were filling with blood. Blood foamed out of his blow hole as he breathed his last breath. Gently, the family let him return to the ocean, all the while wondering why the great boat and net had taken away so many and then thrown back the bodies of their own kin. They couldn't know that the fishermen set the big nets over the dolphins to catch the tuna for food because the tuna liked to travel under the dolphins as they swam. The fishermen could detect the presence of the tuna with their own crude, mechanical sonar devices on their boats. How sad that they could not detect how cruel their methods were to the dolphins, innocent victims of their desire for quick, easy catches!

Nick-Nick thought of the boy in the small boat who had saved him and played with his family in the water. He wondered what kind of people were on the great boat that had killed so many dolphins.

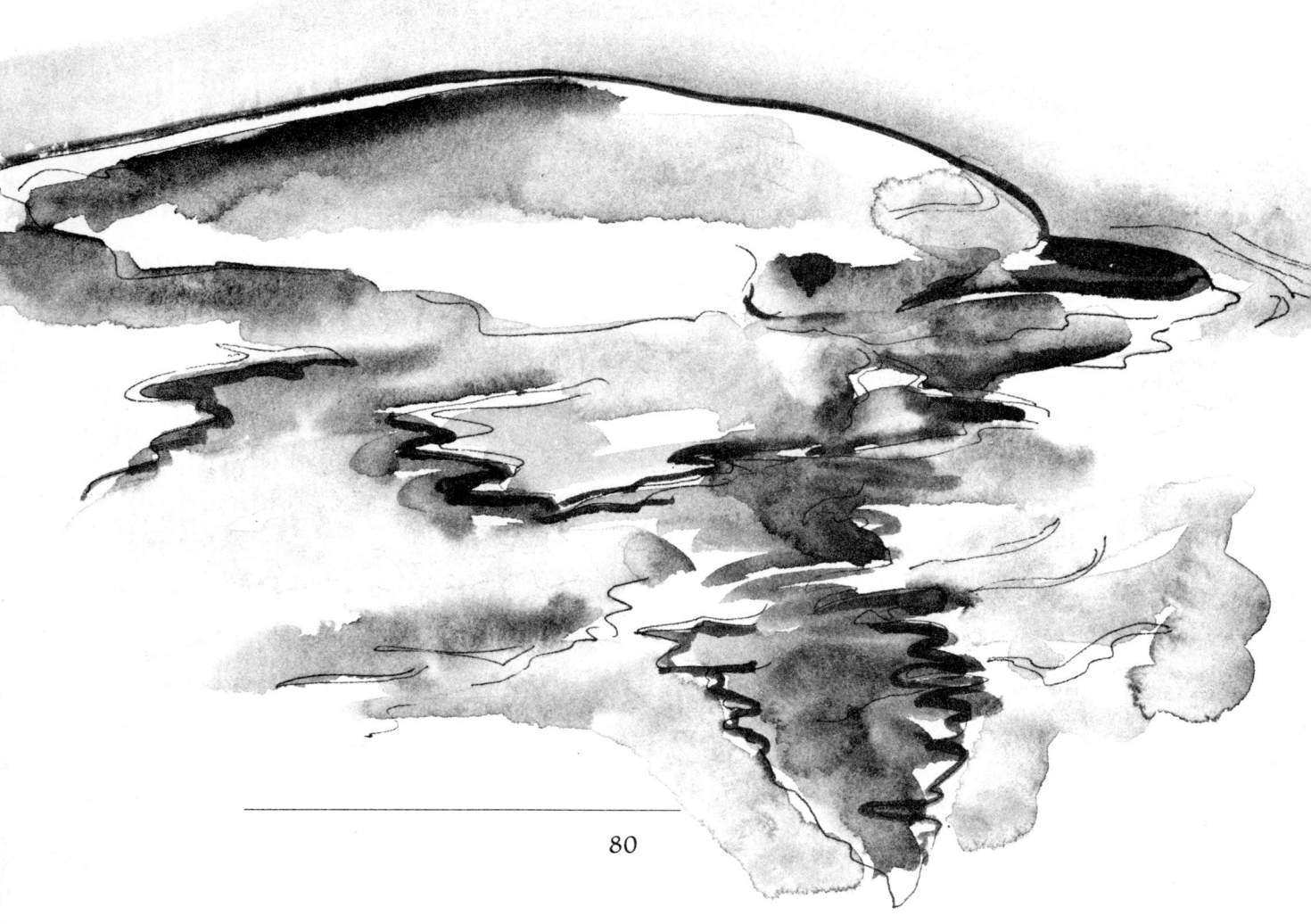

The Giant Net

As they circled the dying dolphins, the family heard a distress call: "Seenaa, Seenaa." The call was weak and plaintive, sinking slowly into the ocean depths. Nick-Nick raced to help the drowning dolphin, with his mother and father close behind him. Though Seenaa was a stranger to them, they could not help but try to save her.

They pushed her to the water's surface so she could recover from the stunning blows she had received in her struggle in the net. When Seenaa was able, once again, to swim on her own, they all left the sad hole of silence and suffering that the fishermen had made in the ocean and returned, once again, to the coastline.

Seenaa would become one of their family and Nick-Nick sensed that she would share his life with her in a special way from now on. They were meant to be mates and to fill their own special roles in the life of the sea.

The Way Of The Dolphin

The family crossed behind the wake of a hundred or more gray whales on their annual trip from the Arctic seas to where they would raise their own whale families. The whales and dolphins traveled back to familiar waters and to safety.

As they drew close to the coast, Seenaa and Nick-Nick rose out of the water and stood on their flukes, belly to belly, happy to be alive. Despite their grief, they were still part of the eternal cycle of life. Wherever there were dolphins there would always be loving and intelligent life on earth.

POSTSCRIPT

Dolphins have many wonderful qualities developed over the generations to aid them in their life in the sea.

At one time, the ancestors of the dolphin lived on the land. For some unknown reason, the dolphins and their cousins the whales, returned to the sea. They learned to hold their breath for longer and longer periods of time and their bodies adapted to withstand the stress of changing water pressure as they plunged deep into the ocean. Dolphins evolved the capability to adapt to water pressures that would kill a human diver if he were not in a pressurized suit.

The Way Of The Dolphin

In the dark, often murky waters, dolphins could not see clearly, so they had to develop a better way to keep in touch with each other, to know where they were going and what might be ahead of them. Dolphins learned to use their voices to tell other dolphins how they felt, to signal important messages ("Dive now!" or "Look out, sharks!") and, perhaps, exchange ideas. They also have a special ultrasonic sonar voice that they can use the way we use radar. When they beep out a series of pulsing sounds, the sounds bounce back a shadow picture of whatever solid object is in front of them. Their brains can translate this picture through this special hearing sense. It's almost like x-ray vision. So, no matter how dark the water may be, the dolphins always know what is ahead of them, down to small details.

Postscript

In such ways does a creature of the land adapt himself to a new environment and become the remarkable animal we know as the dolphin.

The Way Of The Dolphin

Dolphin Anatomy

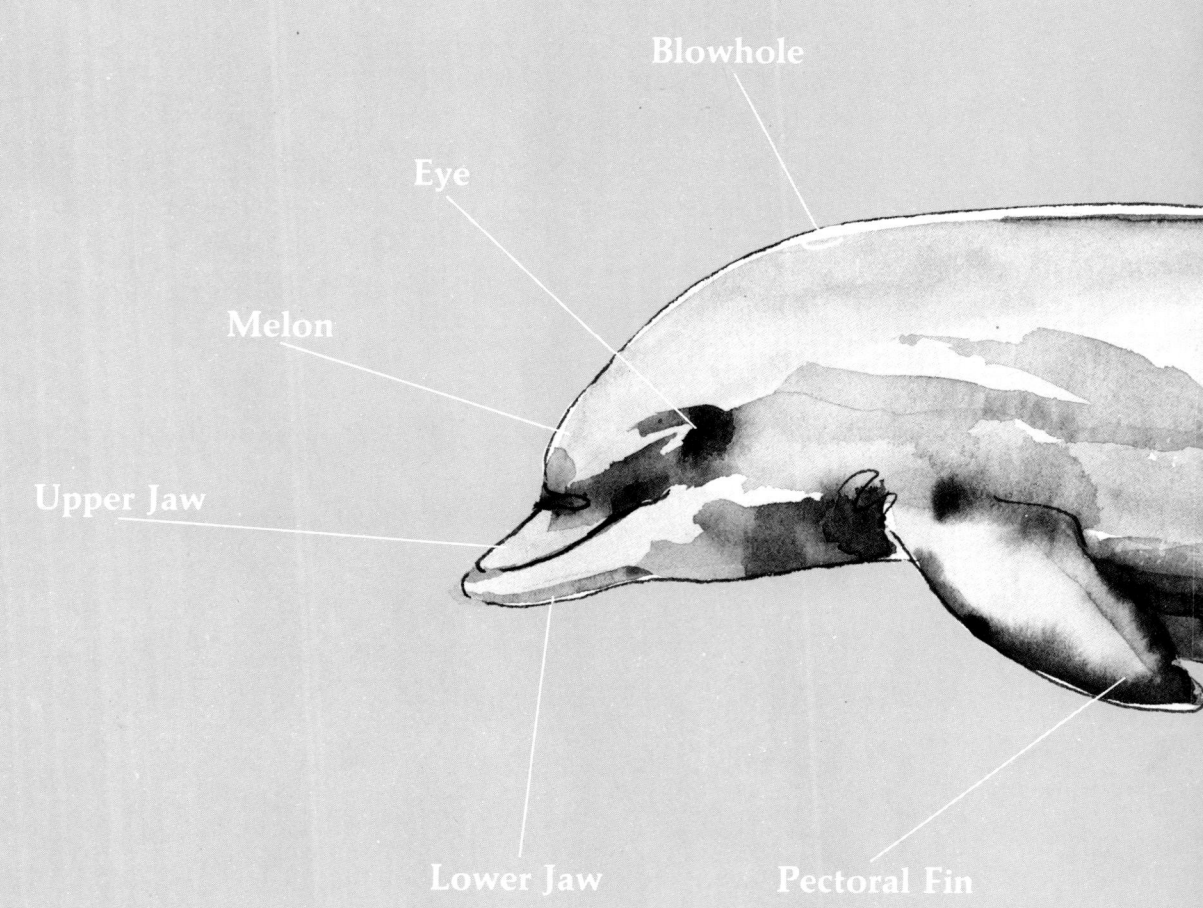

Dolphin Anatomy

The Way Of The Dolphin
Dolphin Sonar

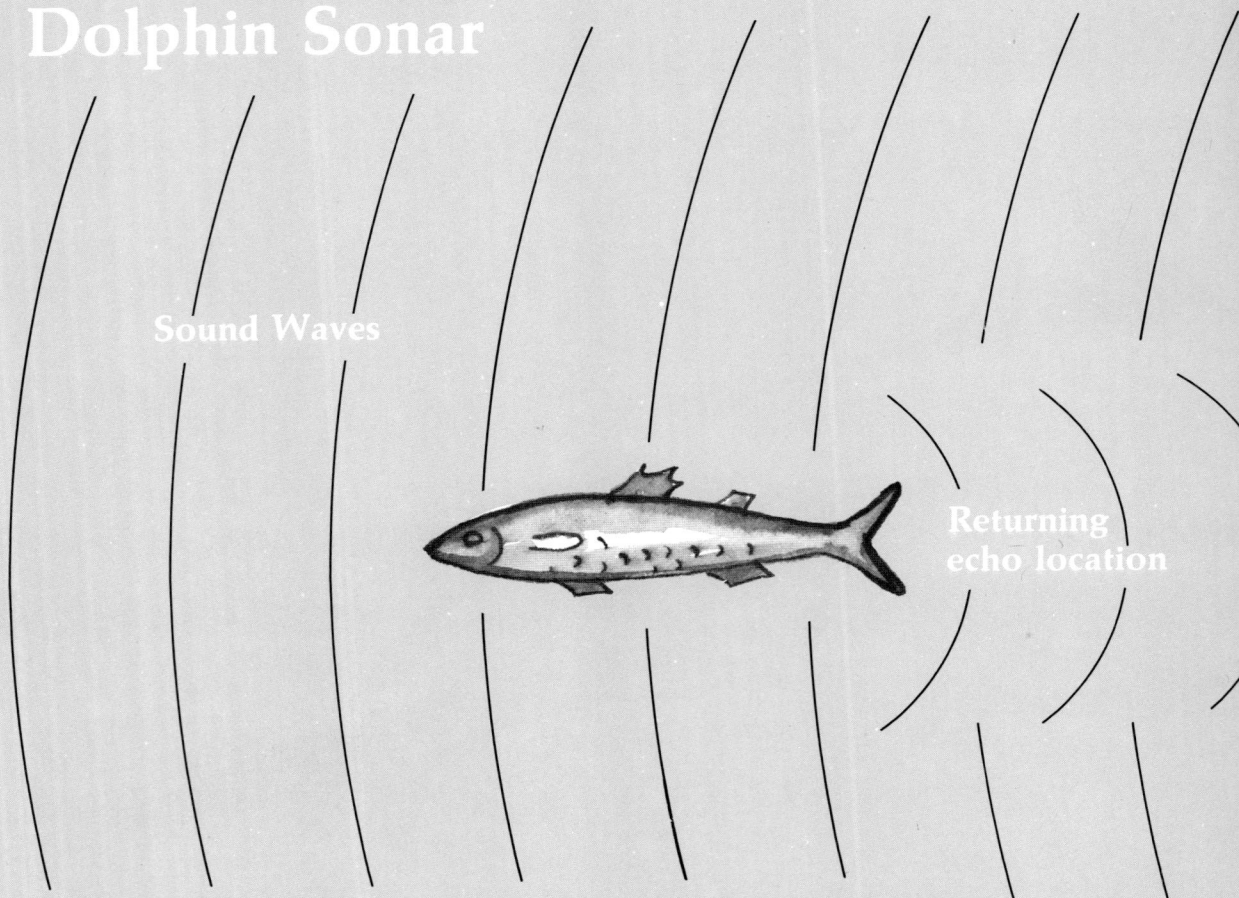

The dolphin sends out clicking sounds by forcing air under pressure from two air sacs and through the fatty melon. Returning echos are transmitted through the lower jaw to the inner ear. High pitched sounds mean the target is close and low pitched sounds mean the target is distant.

Sonar

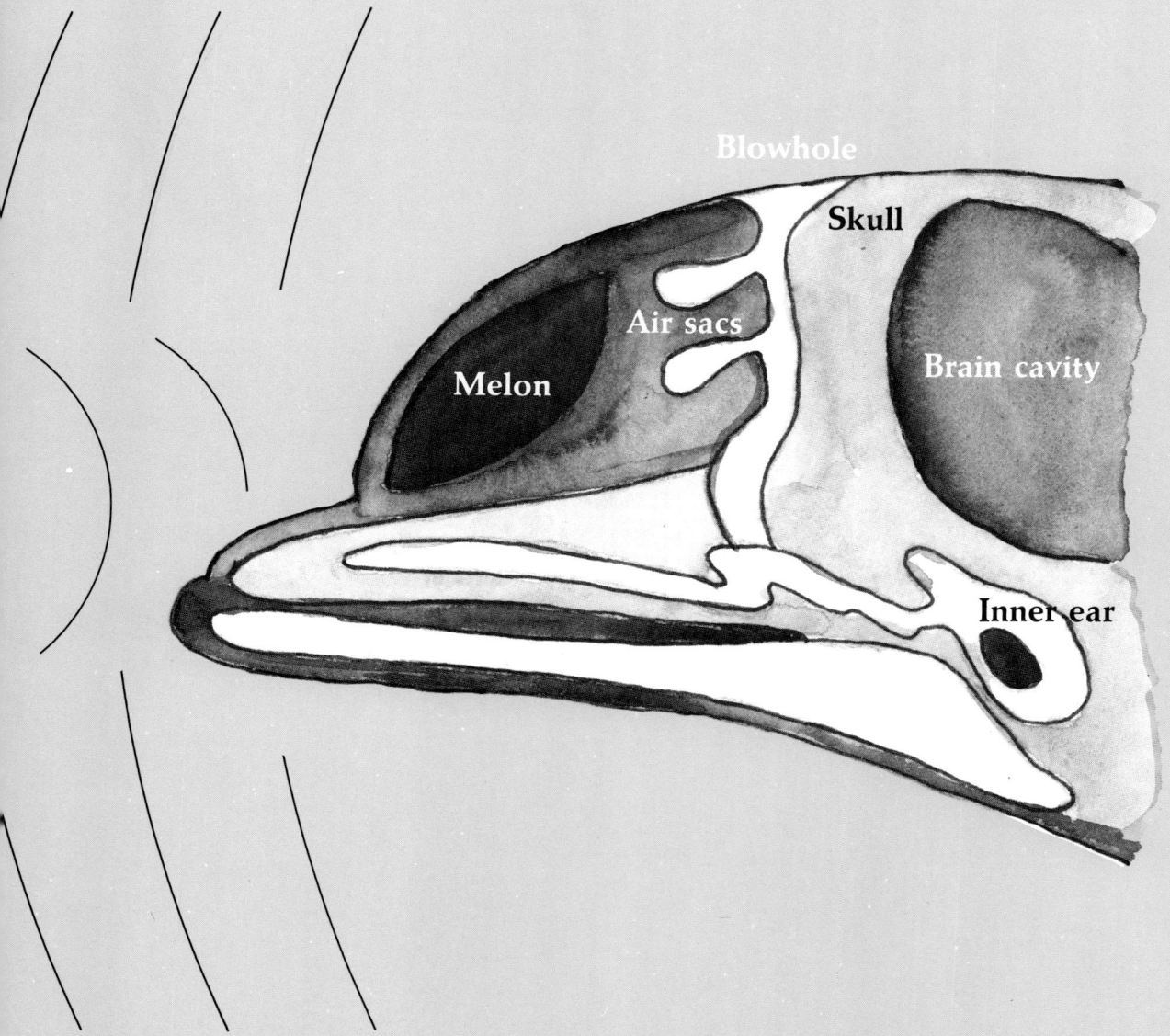

The Way Of The Dolphin

Food Chain in the Life of a Dolphin

"The water swelling up from the depths brought with it decayed material, called ooze, from the bottom of the ocean. The ooze was food for the trillions of microscopic plants and animals, called plankton, that multiplied in these waters, creating a rich soup of nutrients. The plankton was consumed by other microscopic creatures—krill, baby crabs and jellyfish—who in turn, were eaten by small fish, part of the never-ending cycle of ocean life."

Ooze   Plankton   Krill   Mullet

Cycle of Ocean Life

Glossary

abalone — a rock-clinging mollusk or mussel-like creature whose shell is lined with mother-of-pearl.

albatross — a web-footed seabird with a great wingspan that enables it to glide for hundreds of miles.

ambergris — a waxy substance from the sperm whale's intestines which is used as a fixative by the perfume industry.

bottle-nosed dolphin — also called a porpoise, of which there are various species which have a prominent beak and teeth.

eel — a snake-like, smooth-skinned fish

fathom — a unit of length measuring 6 ft. used to measure depth of water.

flying fish — there are several different species all of which have well-developed pectoral fins so they can skim or fly over the surface of the water.

Glossary

gray whale — a large whalebone or baleen whale of the northern Pacific. (Baleen is a horny substance found in two rows of thin plates in the whale's mouth through which it filters its food and which were once used to make corsets or "staves.")

jellyfish — a free swimming marine creature that has a nearly transparent, saucer-shaped body, and tentacles studded with stinging cells.

kelp — also called sea otter's cabbage, a large, brown seaweed that grows to a great length in the ocean forming dense underwater "forests."

killer whale — or Orca, a black and white, flesh-eating whale that hunts in groups called "pods."

krill — minute shell-fish or crustaceans, called plankton, which constitute the principle food of baleen whales.

lagoon — a shallow pool or inlet of water.

mackerel — there are many species, the Spanish mackerel being common in the Pacific; these are large fish that often appear in huge schools.

mullet — there are many species of this perch-like fish throughout the world, which live in schools and suck food off the bottom of shallow waters.

mussel — a double-shelled mollusk that attaches itself to rocks and weeds in the sea.

ooze — a soft deposit of mud, slime, decaying shells, plants, etc.

phosphorescent — a glowing light emitted by many plants and animals.

plankton — the minute plant and animal life present in all sea water.

sea otter — a furry mammal of the Pacific coast that is now endangered by pollution, human interference and competition with abalone fishermen.

sonar x-ray vision — dolphins give very high pitched sounds that bounce off objects in front of them. Dolphins are able to read the echo that bounces back and can make a picture out of the sound waves. Hence, they can "see" in dark and muddy water. Such sonar or sound pictures are now used by doctors to examine patients and are safer than actual x-rays.

spawn — this is the passing and fertilizing of eggs by fish when they reproduce.

sperm whale — a large, toothed whale that has a large closed cavity in its head containing oil and waxy spermaceti used in cosmetics.

winch — a powerful machine with a rotating drum that can pull in a line of rope or cable.